THE HOW TO BE YOU
HANDBOOK

THE HOW TO BE YOU HANDBOOK

Finding your beauty, truth and self-worth

Tisa Mendoza

TATE PUBLISHING
AND ENTERPRISES, LLC

The How to Be You Handbook
Copyright © 2013 by Tisa Mendoza. All rights reserved.

No part of this publication may be reproduced, stored in a retrieval system or transmitted in any way by any means, electronic, mechanical, photocopy, recording or otherwise without the prior permission of the author except as provided by USA copyright law.

The opinions expressed by the author are not necessarily those of Tate Publishing, LLC.

This book is designed to provide accurate and authoritative information with regard to the subject matter covered. This information is given with the understanding that neither the author nor Tate Publishing, LLC is engaged in rendering legal, professional advice. Since the details of your situation are fact dependent, you should additionally seek the services of a competent professional.

Published by Tate Publishing & Enterprises, LLC
127 E. Trade Center Terrace | Mustang, Oklahoma 73064 USA
1.888.361.9473 | www.tatepublishing.com

Tate Publishing is committed to excellence in the publishing industry. The company reflects the philosophy established by the founders, based on Psalm 68:11,
"The Lord gave the word and great was the company of those who published it."

Book design copyright © 2013 by Tate Publishing, LLC. All rights reserved.
Cover design by Allen Jomoc
Interior design by Joana Quilantang

Published in the United States of America

ISBN: 978-1-62510-095-5
1. Self-Help / Personal Growth / Self-Esteem
2. Self-Help / Motivational & Inspirational
13.05.15

Dedication

I dedicate this book to my son, Nathan.

When Nathan was born and looked into my eyes for the first time, I knew he truly saw me. As we gazed into one another's eyes, I was in awe of the knowledge he had brought with him. It was a moment where time and space ceased to exist, and I was fully present to his infinite beauty and to mine. This tiny and amazing being that I held in my arms reminded me that we all begin as pure and flawless, and that we are naturally loving and lovable.

I will always cherish that moment where two perfect, loving beings marveled at each other. You, Nathan, continue to challenge me to allow you to be you, and for me to be me.

This dedication would be incomplete without mentioning my Self.

You've come a long way, Adorable. This is for you, too.

Acknowledgements and Gratitude

A special acknowledgment is due to Marshall Rosenberg and his work on nonviolent communication. Thank you for doing the work that brings wisdom and healing to so many.

A special thank you to Marilyn Kentz, the person who, years ago, first started to coax this book out of me. Writing out all the pain I had experienced in my life was incredibly healing for me, and I think you knew I had to do this before I could produce the book I am able to share today. I have so much love for you, Marilyn. Thank you.

Thank you to Catherine Gonick, who helped me get to the core of my practices and the principles of Be You. Throughout this process, we shared a lot together, including our own personal stories and experiences. Thank you for being more than an editor. Your love, support, and wisdom saw me through. I am grateful to have you as a friend in my life.

Thank you to Marshall Mermell, for giving me the pep talk at "our spot" that I needed to stay on track and complete this book. Taking the pledge with you to complete it was powerful indeed. You reminded me that it was already inside me, a truth I need to be reminded of.

I acknowledge and thank my adorable parents, Georgia Ruby and Getulio, for your undying love and support. You have both taught me so much and continue to give me so much from an unlimited source of love and grace. I love you both so much.

Thank you to my siblings, Tony, Sergio, and Felicia. I was lucky enough to have special relationships and special "moments in time" with you that I cherish. It could be a song or the way the sky looks that brings on memories of times we've shared.

A special thank you to my sister, Felicia, for supporting me and believing in me. I know you've only wished for me to be happy and fulfilled. I love you so much and appreciate how much we share with each other.

To my nephews Sergio, Tyler, and Matthew. I love each of you and am so proud of you and what you each bring into the world. You are in my heart as I launch this book and produce the Be You campaign. I want you each to follow your dreams and live in love with your life every day.

I want to give a special acknowledgement and gratitude to my niece Sable, whom I call a goddess-daughter. Sable, it was you who inspired me the most, early on. I wanted so much for you to experience a life without the pain of feeling worthless. You were only seven when you gave me my first lesson in how I should live. You were the reason I knew I had to get my life together by truly loving my Self, so I could model that for you. It was for you, even before it was for my Self, that I had to learn how to watch my thoughts, the words that I spoke and were spoken about me, and how I treated my Self. We have something very special between us that I cherish. I love you so much—as you are. My only wish for my only baby girl is that you see in your Self what I see.

To Leslie Farrar, my "soul sister conjoined at the heart," the one who never left my side. We never got the operation! In my darkest hour, you saved my life by bringing me back to me. You were my lifeline so many times over. There are no words that come close to the deep gratitude and love I have for you. Thank you for always providing a safe place for me to be me, free of judgment and filled with compassion, empathy, honesty and love. What more can I possibly say other than the obvious: I love you.

To Jason Bastin, I am so grateful to have you in my life. Your love and adoration toward me have taught me so much about my Self and has challenged me to love my Self even more deeply. You have challenged me to love my Self in a way no other person has. I believe I would not have been able to *truly* love my Self without the love you have shown and continue to show me. I love you and am eternally grateful to you.

Last, but not least, I wish to acknowledge Jan-Hendrik Mangold, my best friend in life until the end of this lifetime and not just because you're Nathan's father. You helped me get to me faster. I have so much respect and admiration for you. The way you loved me and saw me gave me permission to be me and proved I was worthy of love. I didn't have to do anything to, or become anything more, than my Self for you to love me. I referred to my Self as damaged goods, and you saw beyond my experiences and loved me as I am. Our love between each other transcends what I thought was possible. Thank you.

Table of Contents

Introduction ------------------------------------- 13
How to Use This Book ------------------------- 19
The Quest for Who I Really Am Begins ---------- 25
What Loving My Self Has Done for Me --------- 29
What Loving Your Self Will Do for You ---------- 39
Thinking Be You --------------------------------- 41
Speaking Be You --------------------------------- 61
Living Be You ------------------------------------ 89
The Forty-Day Be You Program ----------------- 93

Introduction

Our current state of global consciousness, or perhaps I should say unconsciousness, has been a main motivation to write this book. We are living in a time when humanity can either choose to continue bringing about devastating global conflict and the destruction of the environment, or create a truly sustainable, thriving planet based on the practice of Self-love. Changing global consciousness is not easy. It must be done one person at a time, yet there are already many with positive awareness who are making progress toward change. What might happen if we believed we're here to share the fruits of our planet through a collective labor of love, one that began with a practice that enabled us to first love our Selves and then each other? We'd experience harmony and peace, be able to express our needs and cooperate, rather than fight for them to be met.

The good news is that such a practice already exists and can be expressed in just two words: Be You. All that's required to Be You is to learn to treat yourself with healthy doses of Self-love. The practice of Self-love starts with simply accepting yourself as you are, not what the media, other people, or your own inner critics say you should be. It means accepting the larger, unrestricted Self that you were born with and can be. Your Self is naturally abundant, creative and loving. You can think of it as your inner source of power, always there to be drawn on.

Some of us have already embarked on the journey of Self-love necessary to change ourselves and the world. Others are still sleepwalking. If you feel you are beginning to awaken to your inner, powerful Self, rather than try to wake others, all you need to do is Be You. This way you can model a life that others can choose to live when they are ready.

Another motivation for writing is to share the fruits of the pain I experienced as a young woman with other women, especially with young women who are just beginning their journey toward Self and may be struggling. I am a survivor of gang-rape at fifteen, and of bulimia, a violent boyfriend, and suicidal depression in my later teens and early twenties. I've over-exercised, been obsessed with getting a boob job, and have felt driven to obtain the material possessions and seeming good fortune that I envied in others. Today, in my forties, I'm at peace with myself and know that my feelings of self-trust and self-worth are my true source of abundance. Along the way, I developed the practices of Self-love that you will find in this book.

I began to heal in my mid-twenties, by participating in organizations devoted to helping others, especially young people, reading as many inspirational self-help books as I could find, attending workshops and seminars on neurolinguistics and self-actualization, experiencing hypnotherapy, and finding alternative health care practitioners who helped restore both my body and mind.

Slowly, laboriously, and not without further pain, I achieved my own daily practices for achieving Self-love, which I now consider the starting point for being able to help and love others.

During this time, I also worked in and left the corporate world, started a radio show and almost a TV show, married and gave birth to my wonderful son, Nathan, who has been my foremost ongoing inspiration.

In 2003, I was introduced to a process of nonviolent communication, which is also known as "compassionate communication," and began practicing it five years ago. It was developed and is taught by Marshall Rosenberg, an international expert in conflict resolution and communication and founder of the international organization, Center for Nonviolent Communication, www.cnvc.org.

I support a vision of living with my fellow human beings as explained on Marshall's website, where he states that nonviolent communication is not new, but is based on achieving the natural state of compassion where no violence is present in the heart. Nonviolent communication reminds us of what we already instinctively know—how good it feels to authentically connect to another human being. By teaching us to hear our own deeper needs and those of others, it allows us to discover the depth of our own compassion and to become aware that all human beings are only trying to honor universal values and needs, every minute of the day. Do you desire to exist this way? I do. I want to relearn my intrinsic nature and to be authentic, compassionate, and loving in all I do.

In 2006, my new beliefs and practices culminated in my founding of Buzzledom, Inc., a company whose vision statement is "media with purpose" and whose mission statement is "We give good buzz." I created this company as my way of adding positivity to the planet. Rather than complaining about the messages put out by the media, I would produce my own. I also wanted to introduce a business model in which part of the profits would be donated back into the community. The proceeds from this handbook will help support the campaign closest to my heart, called Be You: Love Your Self, Love Your Life! The Be You campaign is aimed at helping as many people as possible develop the kind of Self-love that will allow them to better connect with Self, others, and the planet—in the healthiest ways for mind, body and spirit. The ultimate goal is to promote a sense of happiness, well-being, and fulfillment of Self that I believe is everyone's birthright.

By launching the Be You! Campaign and writing this book, I hope to make it easier for you to achieve your birthright.

If you are in search of your Self, this handbook is specifically designed to help you navigate through all the messages and conversations in your life that tell you the opposite of being amazing and perfect as you are. My hope is that the practices and personal experiences I share will allow you to fully embrace and celebrate your Self, while combating the limited views of both men and women portrayed in the media, and the limiting beliefs in our society that hinder our appreciation of ourselves and others. For everyone who reads this, and especially young women, it's time to deprogram and reconnect with our individual strengths so that, together, we live more fulfilling lives.

How to Use This Book

This section of the book includes a pledge to your Self, followed by the ten principles of Be You. Next, you will find more about my experiences, provided for whatever light they might shed on yours. Then come sections called Thinking Be You, Speaking Be You, and Living Be You; and finally, a forty-day program based on the ten Be You principles. I recommend reading everything in order. The pledge and the principles will prepare you for the three Be You sections, which provide information on how to put the principles into practice. You can then use the practices and tips you've learned in these sections in conjunction with the forty-day program. If after reading the pledge, you wish to take it immediately, please do. Or you can wait until you've read the rest of the book and decide to start the program.

Once you've read the whole book, I also recommend that you keep it handy. It's provided in a compact format so you can refer to it whenever you need a reminder of how to Be You or find your Self getting pulled into old, limiting thought and language patterns. The principles provide a quick reference to keep you on track. Take a deep breath before reading one or all of them, and take a moment for the conscious and subconscious parts of your mind to accept what you read as truth.

Let's begin, with:

The Be You Pledge

On this day, I, [your name], pledge to accept, honor, love and respect my Self as I am, and you as You are. Therefore, I …

- speak gently about my Self and body, as well as those of others;
- treat my Self and others with respect;
- am grateful for my body's amazing senses, which allow me to experience the joys of seeing, hearing, smelling, tasting, and touching;
- eat guilt-free, with joy and gratitude;
- listen to my inner truth and body;
- feed my body healthy, fresh, unprocessed food and organic foods when available;
- appreciate that my body, mind and spirit allow me every experience in life and an opportunity to learn to love my Self and others more deeply;
- express my Self with authenticity;
- accept and honor my Self and others.

The commitment to your Self begins when you take the pledge. This act that you take for your Self is the start of changing limiting patterns so that you can live your life in fulfillment and joy. You can take it at any time. When you do, I encourage you to join others who have taken it on the Be You campaign's website, www.beyoucampaign.com.

May you acknowledge the power source within you, and remember to give your Self compassion and love daily.

The principles of Be You are very simple and become easier to apply the more you practice them:

The Ten Principles of Be You

Relearning how to be you is a lifestyle change and the following principles will help you get back to you on the occasions when you fall out of alignment with your natural state of being powerful and knowing that you have everything it takes as you are. These principles are to serve you as reminders. These are tools for you to draw upon when you stagger on your path. Think of them as a fresh drink of water or walking stick along your inner path to Self-love.

1. I am born with everything needed to fulfill my desires. The only things preventing me from fulfilling my desires are the subconscious thoughts and

beliefs that counter this truth. I release all subconscious and conscious thoughts that prevent me from believing that I am less than perfect as I am in this moment.

2. I accept everything about myself, including my physical body, to the choices I have made in my past experiences and any hurt and pain I may have caused others. I choose to speak gently about my Self and others.

3. I am grateful for my wonderful senses that allow me to see, hear, smell, taste, touch, and feel. I will notice my sensory experiences throughout this day and give thanks for each sense.

4. I allow my Self to be and I allow others to be. I only have to be responsible for my Self and present to the existence of others. I have no need to be responsible for how others feel. I allow them to feel what they feel and I will authentically express my feelings and needs with them as we experience life with each other.

5. I am a human being capable of giving and receiving love. I do not label myself as good or bad; I am simply the essence of where possibility begins. This is true for my Self and for my fellow human beings. I choose to see my Self and others as worthy and deserving.

The How to Be You Handbook

6. I am authentic. It is in my nature to have feelings and desires. I am capable of expressing my feelings and needs. I am capable of being present to the feelings and needs of others, and am able to look beyond any limiting belief or illusion that someone may have about who I am or who they think they are.

7. I am compassionate. I am able to give compassion to my Self and others. I will listen with an open heart and be completely present to others. I will not be offended or take things personally; this is an old practice that I am releasing and replacing with compassion.

8. I have the ability to overcome negative feelings including anger, resentment, despair, hate, loneliness and all forms of fear. When these feelings come up, I know they are there for me to resolve and heal, so that I can experience higher, positive feelings that expand my experience. I am capable of overcoming anything I put my attention to. I am fully capable, wise and strong.

9. I am here to experience loving relationships with others and know that I must have, or desire to have, a healthy and loving relationship with my Self. My relationships with others create opportunities to see my Self and to love my Self and others more deeply.

10. I surrender to the flow of love that resides within me. Love has always been with me. It has never been necessary for someone to give it to me, and I have not needed to receive love from someone else in order to give it. I now open my heart and allow love to flow through me.

The Quest for Who I Really Am Begins

When I was twenty-five years old and a newlywed, I had a small epiphany. It was the slightest, silliest thing, yet it made me aware of something big. There were certain things that my mother did, especially when it came to household duties, that I had adopted as my own, as if by osmosis. She cooked eggs every morning and, after cracking them open, would put the cracked shells back in the carton. Now that I was living in my own home, I did the same thing until one day when my sister-in-law paid a visit.

I still remember her yelling at me from the kitchen, "Tisa, what are you doing? Why do you have all these cracked shells in the egg carton?" I didn't have an answer. As I thought about it, shocked that apparently this was not what everyone did, I was left with *OMG, what else am I doing without knowing why?*

Later, I learned that my mother left the cracked shells in the carton because we didn't have a garbage disposal. Keeping the shells refrigerated, until garbage day, kept our garbage bag from smelling any more than it had to. It was then I first realized that much of what I did was based on other people's beliefs and habits, and that I was probably unconscious of most of them. After this, I started noticing and questioning the various beliefs I had acquired, aware that they could have been very different if I'd had different parents.

This epiphany was just a piece of the fractured puzzle, not my big moment about who I really am. At that moment, I had little idea of who I was or would become. I began noticing and questioning everything I did, and asking if there were better ways of doing them. I first noticed that imitating my mother didn't end with egg cartons. My entire kitchen was set up like hers. I changed it by moving the dish rack to a new location. I saw that I'd also patterned my limited palate on hers. She was a picky eater, who rarely tried new foods. I became more open to them. It was through small steps like these that my quest for who I really am started.

My steps had to be small. Even though I was now supposedly an adult, I was really still a child, a cracked shell myself, dealing with overwhelming issues. I was battling my own negative inner voices and the judgments I believed everyone had toward me. I was not yet aware that I had an eating disorder, or that my suicidal depression and low self-esteem had anything to do with the gang-rape and abusive boyfriend I suffered when I was a teenager. I wasn't yet ready to question my beliefs about my distorted body image or why I wasn't happy. It was going to be a long time before I gained enough experience, wisdom, and self-actualization to get to who I really am through the practice of Self-love. As I eventually discovered, learning how to love your Self goes beyond acquiring self-esteem and self-confidence. Loving your Self gives you the strength of Self-worth.

Loving your Self is a process. We never go through life thinking we need to get to know ourselves more deeply, in fact, we are mostly taught that we need to make ourselves better. It's in our media, on our playgrounds, in our own homes—this perpetuating message that we are not enough. We are not told that we are worthy and deserving. We are taught to search for love from someone else, rather than give it to ourselves first. So I'm telling you, I'm reminding you that the only kind of love that matters is having unconditional love toward your Self. And the sooner that you believe that it is your birthright to be, do, and have all that you desire, the better everyone's life experience will be too.

What Loving My Self Has Done for Me

Let me further introduce my Self:

My full name is Theresa Anne Mendoza, but I go by Tisa, a nickname given to me by my mother before I was born. It's pronounced like Lisa with a T and I love it, though people sometimes need a few attempts and reminders to get the pronunciation right. Some rarely do and insist my name is Tish or Tina. When I got to first grade and encountered another Theresa, it felt natural to become Tisa for good, and that's what I still like to be called. So let me say:

Hi, my name is Tisa.

Now that I love my Self, I also love Tisa, as she was and who she is. I accept the choices that were made for her when she was too young to make them for herself and the choices I have made since then. As I did in the Dedication, which you may have thought seemed strange, I can now call myself:

Adorable

Let me explain why I do. For years, I thought of myself as anything but adorable because I was filled with self-hatred for the way I looked and the life I was born into. Today, I think of adorable as describing any person or animal you know and love as a newborn, with the kind of radical cuteness you can't resist. You not only can't resist, you are drawn in, feeling the awe of helpless love mixed with a desire to play with this adorable creature. Now, imagine feeling this way toward your Self. This Self is not only the open, unrestricted one we are all capable of realizing as individuals, it's the one we all share because we're interconnected.

Finally being able to declare I am adorable gives me feelings of peace and tranquility—also of gratitude, and a base-level contentedness with what I am. I have learned to embrace my adorable Self even as I feel and express frustration and anger. Think of an adorable two-year-old who is just learning to use her will. She may say no a hundred times in an hour and then throw a tantrum when she gets too tired to continue. But although she can be trying, she's still adorable, right?

Today, I am a practitioner of Self-love and a warrior for the preservation of Self. I am grateful to be where I am because I know that my peace and serenity comes from my acceptance and still-growing awareness of who I truly am. I have people in my life who love me for who I am, unconditionally, and feeling good with my Self and others is how I wish to spend my time. I no longer choose to do things solely out of obligation. I prefer to spend little to no time with people who may judge me and my choices, but I accept where they are in their lives and keep my heart open toward them. I no longer feel responsible for other people's feelings; I simply practice empathy and provide compassion. Is it easy? No, especially when things happen that trigger feelings of dissatisfaction or unmet needs. Then I need to remember to give my Self empathy and compassion, to treat my Self gently and proceed with caution, and this does get easier with practice. As my genuine Self-love grows deeper, the less difficulty I have in encounters with others. Also, I can often say about myself:

I feel yummy.

This too may sound strange, but yummy is what I call the feeling of perfect bliss that can sometimes come from food. Most food lovers will understand what I mean. Yummy to me is a bite into a moist Red Velvet cupcake or the deep appreciation of a heavenly forkful of cheesy, meaty, lasagna. Yummy is about the engagement of the senses. It's being present to only the moment, of experiencing and appreciating deliciousness. Think about how grateful you are when encountering a delicious mouthful of food. Like an adorable infant, you feel completely alive and full of well-being because you are getting exactly what you need, and all of your senses are experiencing pleasure and fulfillment. It's possible to feel the same way about your Self, as you enjoy the deliciousness of simply being, in many different moments.

To me, feeling yummy is the opposite of feeling bulimic. Having experienced and gotten past the pain of bulimia, I know the difference between eating for nourishment and eating as a desperate act to fill my empty void and escape discomfort. I've also learned that just as with food, I can choose what I put into my Self, starting with my beliefs and intentions. I can choose to align my Self with thoughts and actions that nurture and allow me to grow and connect with others, or I can stay aligned with old, unconscious beliefs that keep me stunted and disconnected.

Today, just as I nurture and give attention to those I love, I do the same for my Self. I truly love my Self, and it is this love that has led to what has most profoundly changed my life: my ability to trust my Self. No matter how much pain I was in, I was always able to give some love to others and to help the underdog. Now that I can love and trust my Self, I can take my past passions and experiences and use them for the benefit of others. I can act from where I am, without the need to make myself over in a hopeless attempt to achieve perfection. Today I can say:

I love my Self…just as I am.

I can also say:

I am worthy…just as I am.

When I began my search, I had a difficult time believing that I could actually connect with my inner source of power. The books I was reading assured me it was there and, that according to the discoveries of quantum physics, was one with the energy that powered the universe. My inner source was part of a unified field of energy-making probabilities, meaning my Self had infinite potential and possibilities. Later experiences of body-work, via the powerful chiropractic technique called Network Spinal Analysis, allowed me to understand this more deeply. I realized that aligning my body could be a way of aligning my Self. I began to accept my gut feelings of "just knowing," and saw clearly how so many of us live misaligned to our basic needs, desires, and innate ability to heal ourselves.

I envisioned how we are all connected through the seemingly empty space between atoms that is really full of interconnected energy and holds us together as a single operating unit. Just as cell phones and wireless laptops connect through the energy of electricity, we connect through a grid of make-it-happen energy that is constantly working for us and has our backs. I recognized that to bring about positive change, we need only align our lives with this greater energy, in body, mind, spirit, thoughts, words and action. A few well-chosen tools can help us optimize our interconnection. And to begin to do this, we need only believe this connecting energy is there.

I also learned what people have been saying for thousands of years that intention, thoughts and even prayers can change reality. This sounded bizarre at first, yet in the twenty or so years since I set out on my journey, neuroscience has been providing the evidence. We know now that intentions and beliefs can actually change how the brain functions, and also the body. Body, mind, and spirit truly can be addressed as one reality in ways that can improve reality. Your reality. It is an exciting time to be alive, and an especially exciting time to Be You.

How much of your reality can you truly change? If you're wondering just how much of mine I've changed, I would say the shift has been radical and life-altering. Ask if I always feel good, and the answer is no. Life is always a mixture of darkness and light, of feeling satisfaction when our needs are met and discomfort when they're not, and all of it must in its own way be honored. I will say I am now in a place in my life where I choose to fully express my Self. At one time, I only thought I understood what this means, but now understand it as actively making sure I am in alignment with my amazingness, that is, my highest potential for being. I sometimes reach it, and I do my best to stay present to it.

As for my spiritual beliefs, I have no doubt they were influenced by my mother, who influenced so much else in my life. A devout Catholic, she told me that God, our father in heaven who loves us, loves us very much indeed. He is also a forgiving father, she assured me. Do I believe in God in that way? Do I believe in God?

I believe that a greater omnipresent being exists, and like the idea of something bigger than I am watching over and caring for me. I think it's safe to say we were born with free will. I believe we are all born with the same opportunity to make whatever we want out of our lives by choosing the beliefs we hold about our obstacles and struggles. Whatever our challenges, our beliefs are our greatest tool for navigating and overcoming them. For me, hypnotherapy and neuro-linguistic programming showed that whatever we choose to believe becomes our reality. I therefore choose to believe in all the things that can make my experience of life amazing, including that I am the source of this richness.

It was in my darkest hours, as my nerves shredded under the stress of being a young mother and a business owner in a financial crisis, that I first chose what to believe. At the time, it didn't seem like a choice, only what I had to believe to keep from giving up. Yet, choice it was. I knew I could choose to continue believing all the negative messages shrieking within me, in which case I'd stay curled up in a ball in the corner of my room, sobbing, terrified, and unable to take care of my son and my life, or I could focus on what was still possible. Fortunately, I was down so far that up was the only direction I could see. I found my Self reaching for a new reality by somehow making myself believe, in what then seemed like just a bunch of airy-fairy spiritual teachings.

Feeling I was just pretending, I "chose" to believe what the books I'd been reading were telling me, that I was born in the likeness of God or was at least part of some omnipresent being, source or intelligence that had limitless possibilities. I was part of the Divine Source. Feeling I had no choice in the matter, I chose to believe that I was a spiritual being that had decided to live in a human body, to experience life on the other side of the so-called veil. I chose to believe that if I imagined something good, stayed focused on it, and believed I deserved it, that it would eventually manifest in my life. Through my Self, my inner power source, I would always have access to the power of the universe, and the Divine Source, and in turn would be willing to meet me more than halfway. I could have control of my life again, even though right then life was giving me nothing but grief. Who was I kidding? At first, I could barely even think these preposterous things, yet as I learned over time, change really does start with intent, even when you're only wanting to have intent. With enough repetition, I actually began to believe what I was hoping.

As you've seen for yourself, the principles of Be You are simple. It's the practical application of them that's tough—at first. When my practice starts to get difficult, I remind my Self it's tough because I believe it to be so, and then that with a little more practice, I'll get to what I'm seeking. I'm here to tell you, if you just stick with it, it gets easier, and I'm the living proof. As you practice, stay with the core belief that you love and feel good about your Self, and good things will follow. That old cliché is true; Love is the answer. I now believe that Self-love is an even better answer. If you care for your Self as you would for a precious other, your life will evolve. Loving your Self frees you up from judging yourself and others. You learn to embrace change, and to expand your vision far beyond the horizon of limiting beliefs. You feel free to make decisions for your Self because you know you are capable.

I now have no trouble believing I have the power to create anything in my life that I wish, which is why I constantly, and now with less effort, align my thoughts, words and actions to what I most desire—the reality that my inner knowing and spirit, my larger Self, can access at any time. That reality is there for you, and you too could find yourself feeling what I've described as adorable and yummy.

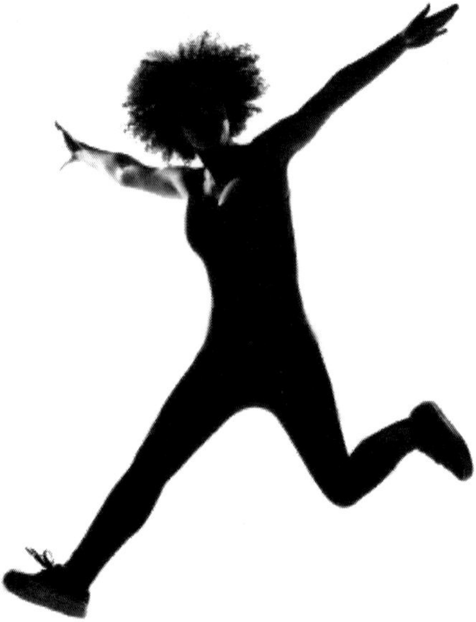

What Loving Your Self Will Do for You

Though we all share a Self that can live with love, wisdom, and joy, getting to it requires a different path for each individual. We must each climb our own mountain, so to speak, and mine may look nothing like yours. Whatever the mountain, however, the same kinds of tools are useful for climbing. Learning to replace negative beliefs with affirmations you believe is like replacing worn-out sneakers with brand-new hiking boots. They'll help you get to the top, and once you're there, you'll see what you've achieved:

The Benefits of Being You

- You feel good about your life.
- You find it easy to be grateful for your life.
- You no longer have the need to fix other people because you have no need to fix your Self.
- You trust your Self.
- You realize there are no irrevocably "bad" choices, as long as you choose from a place of self-love and trust.

- You have clarity, focus, purpose and intention.
- Because you have clarity, you are able to communicate more effectively.
- You communicate with compassion and express your Self authentically.
- Accepting, loving and respecting your Self unconditionally allows you to love and accept others, freeing up your time and energy to focus on what you desire.
- You embrace every aspect of your life, and there are no "bad" experiences, only opportunities in every moment.
- You expect and receive gifts from life every day.
- You no longer choose to do things out of obligation.
- You are gentle toward your Self.
- You no longer take negativity personally.
- You know your Self-worth.
- You live in gratitude and joy.

Does this sound good? You're ready to put on your new boots and take that first step.

Thinking Be You

*I used to think I wasn't beautiful, not like the women
I admired. Now I realize that I, too, am beautiful.*

Why do we need to learn how to think Be You? Because everything, including our beliefs, begin as a thought. Because so many of our thoughts are judgments, which are the hardest thoughts to change whether they are conscious or unconscious. We need to learn how to change unconscious thoughts to overcome judgments and also to get what we really want.

Years ago, I heard a motivational speaker ask why we need to be motivated to achieve something we desire. The answer is that if your conscious mind wants something, but your unconscious mind does not believe in having it, for whatever reason, your unconscious mind will win the argument. That's why affirmations don't always work; your unconscious mind must first agree with them. Moreover, whatever is in your unconscious mind usually got there a long time ago and carved out deep neuronal patterns that resist change. As the motivational speaker went on to explain, negative thoughts get installed when we're very young, because we are told no so many times. One study showed that a toddler can be told no up to four hundred times a day. The usual reason for this is to keep us safe, but as our innate wish to explore makes us reach out for the hot stove and we hear a loud, *no*, we are learning self-doubt.

According to the speaker, due to the way the brain works, it takes many more positive reinforcements than there were negative inputs to undo the damage of early conditioning. And thus, there is hardly a limit to how many times you can use the affirmation, *I am worthy*, or any other. Nor is there a limit to how many times you can tell yourself to Stop Judging.

Like weeds, judgments must be uprooted before affirmations can be planted and flower. Both actions are necessary in the practice of Self-love, which comes down to allowing your Self to Be You and allowing others to be who they are, too.

Yet how often does this happen? Judgment is everywhere, in corporations and nonprofits, government, our communities, schools and playgrounds, in our families, and in our heads. If others aren't doing what we believe is right, in alignment with our beliefs, we consider them wrong. Sometimes we go to war over our judgmental beliefs and kill people on their behalf. And even when we accept that people have different beliefs, we still think ours are the right ones. Nothing gets in the way of a positive affirmation as much as a negative judgment, whether it's coming from outside or we've internalized it. We, therefore, need to transform all our limiting thoughts and beliefs so that our Self can grow.

Many conscious, self-limiting thoughts are fairly obvious, especially when they are judgments voiced by another person. And when you really don't like looking in the mirror, it's fairly easy to guess you might unconsciously believe you're less attractive than you'd like, compared to images of beauty that are prevalent in film, television, and magazines. These limiting images of beauty are offered to us over and over again, unfortunately, leading many of us to unconsciously adopt them as truth. Self-reflection, body-work, psychotherapy, hypnotherapy, neurolinguistics, journaling, and tracking dreams all offer ways to get in touch with your self-limiting thoughts, beliefs, and judgments, including the less obvious ones that lurk below the surface of your mind.

Combating Limiting Thoughts and Beliefs

> It took me a long time not to judge myself through someone else's eyes.
>
> —Sally Field

Here is one way to fight limiting, negative thoughts and beliefs, whether they come from within or from others. First, simply try to notice them. You may be surprised at how many there are. Ask your Self what you are choosing to believe that might be limiting you, and others, from enjoying greater fulfillment. Remind your Self that there are countless ways to deal with what you are thinking. Now, try replacing those beliefs with affirmative thought-forms, mental creations that can aid in the manifestation of positive intent. As you will recall, the power to change your beliefs, and therefore your reality, begins with intent. So, try filling your mind with some of these affirmative thought-forms, starting with:

It is my nature to be capable of achieving anything I desire. I am not a label; I am not my past actions. I am perfect as I am right now. I am acceptance.

In a situation where someone is badgering and judging you, where you are biting your tongue, shutting down, and letting that person tell you what you should be doing, thinking, or feeling, take a deep breath and know in your heart the following:

I am willing to step outside this situation and look at it with a fresh pair of eyes. I know this person is expressing her own inner conflict about who she is and what she believes. I will not allow this experience to close my heart or taint my truth. I offer compassion and genuinely wish that she finds peace within her own heart, so that she sees the truth about who she is. I am compassion.

In a situation where you are fighting with another person and trying to make your own point and feeling angry and resentful, as hard as it may be, stop and take a deep breath. First acknowledge your own anger and any violent thoughts you may have as a result, such as wishing to hit this person. Feel the thought, and let it pass. Then, open your heart and try to think of what that person needs. Most often anger is an expression of not knowing how to say, "I am hurting. I am afraid." When people can't express their true feelings and choose to say hurtful things instead, it is only because they have never seen compassionate communication in action. If the person continues, at this point it would be good to take a deep breath, open your heart even further, and simply desire to change how you feel by reminding your Self:

I am doing my best to heal this situation. I want to resolve this conflict compassionately without judgment. I am accountable for how I have interacted with this person and want to elevate my experience with him for the sake of my own well-being and his.

I know it may be difficult to have compassion for someone who is attacking you, arousing your anger, and feeding your self-doubt. We all battle with self-doubt, which is why a lot of people might challenge what I've just said about using positive thought-forms. They might give me examples of why they are undeserving losers, telling me about how much money they've lost, how they've failed at relationships, and how badly they've treated others. They might be telling you similar things about yourself, yet this doesn't mean that you, or they, are less than a perfect being. You may have made bad decisions and caused hurt, pain, and shame to others, yet this does not alter the fact that you still have the potential to change. The only thing stopping you is what you allow your Self to believe about you.

If nothing else works in the moment, you can always combat a limiting thought with a simple *stop*. Yell to your Self in your head to *stop it*. Then shake off that limiting thought, like you would a bee about to sting you. The important thing is to stop the judging.

If you find that other people's negative judgments and beliefs about you are influencing what you believe about your Self, you can also try limiting your time, or even cutting your ties, with those individuals, at least until you can detach from their judgments. By the same token, you will benefit from hanging out with people whom you admire and who are positive because they will be your strongest advocates and allies.

Thinking Be You means stopping judgment and replacing it with compassion, starting with your Self. Therefore, be generous with giving compassionate thoughts and feelings to your Self. When you make a mistake, rather than beat your Self up, take responsibility for the error, and then give your Self compassion. Sometimes this is difficult, especially if your mistake has caused another person hardship or pain. In that case, you can only do your best to make amends, and then offer your Self compassion.

Here are a few thought-forms that support the intent to have Self-compassion:

Think of your Self as your best friend. Ponder that a minute. It's easy for us to love our friends as they are, so give some of what you feel about your best friend to your Self. Friends rarely intentionally put each other down. They lift up and support each other in times of need.

Think of all your positive attributes. It may seem silly to create a list of things you like about your Self, and it can be a very challenging task if you think there's nothing to like, or that a list of what you don't like about your Self would be ten times longer. Just give it a shot. Think long enough, and you will probably surprise your Self.

Do your best to view your Self as lovable. When I choose to be me, the me that craves to be authentic and loved as I am, I feel fulfilled, content, and happy. I feel able to connect with others more deeply and know that I'm lovable as I am.

As you practice Thinking Be You, you can expect to fall back into negative patterns from time to time. Progress can be two steps forward, one back. At these times, you might notice that you have even more negative judgments about your Self than you thought. You might also notice that you frequently judge other people. We've all done this, but if you find that you always seem to be critiquing others in your mind, it can be painful. Constantly judging others is a pretty reliable sign that you are highly critical of your Self. And, I'd be willing to bet, that you have often felt criticized by people who love you. With a little more practice, you might realize they've criticized you because they've been self-critical, too. Thinking Be You can help to break this cycle of sleepwalking. Again, the best way to begin replacing these negative thoughts is to be gentle with your Self. You can then pay attention to the specifics.

For example, if you have regrets, the thought-form to use is, *I forgive my Self*. And the thought-form, *I'm worthy*, can lead you to Self-forgiveness. Regrets and forgiveness can be tricky, however. Many people don't want to even think of regrets because they believe they haven't suffered enough to merit forgiveness and that receiving it would be a cop-out, especially if there's another person involved who refuses to forgive them. Yet, without the act of Self-forgiveness, you can't open your Self to future opportunities.

Thought-forms are also feelings, and the negative ones that prevent us from being our best Self are those of regret, shame, anger, abandonment, and unworthiness. These are the feelings that lead to further thought-forms known as the *Coulda, Shoulda, Woulda's*, pesky creatures that are hard to get rid of once they appear.

When you are trying to use an affirmative thought-form, remember that affirmations only work as long as you really believe what you are saying. If saying *I am worthy* feels uncomfortable because you believe it's a false statement, then find something else to say that is true. This might be: *I am willing to feel self-worth. I am doing my best to believe I am worthy*. Your deep yearning to realize your intent is what will help you to feel worthy, and whenever you express your Self authentically about your needs, you feel content.

Thinking Be You is about believing that you are worthy and that so is everyone else. It's about replacing judgment with compassion and thinking with the heart. A heart filled with Self-love will naturally overflow, with compassionate thoughts and feelings for your Self and others.

Your Body is a Miracle

Thinking Be You is about Self-acceptance. This includes accepting your Self from your head to your toes, the body you were born with, as it exists today. If, in the past, you've looked in the mirror and pointed out your flaws, wished for eyes or hair of a different color, for fuller breasts, or, if you're a guy, for a more "masculine" physique, it's time to stop these thoughts. Accepting your body does not mean you have to like what you see in the mirror, only that you are no longer going to permit thoughts about it that limit your being.

Here's an exercise for achieving this: Look at your Self in the mirror without judgment. The minute you begin to judge yourself, *stop*. This is a powerful technique which I've used myself. I used to look in the mirror constantly, hate the nose I saw, and become flooded with thoughts about surgery to make it pointier. Same with my boobs, which needed to be bigger. It was a relief to stop thinking about how I could fix all these flaws and just look at my Self, thinking nothing. With practice, I learned how to shut down judging thoughts as they came up, and you will too.

You can learn to look at your body without judging, just as you'd look at anything else. If you're looking at a house, for example, you might note that it's large, pretty, and has extra-nice window treatments, and you therefore like it. Liking the house because it's pretty is a judgment. In this case, it's only a value judgment, reflecting your belief that you value prettiness, but if you were looking at your body and thinking it was not pretty, your next thought would be a moralistic judgment; *what I am seeing is bad.* Rather than go there, you can just stay present to what you see, noting the facts. If you're looking at the house, you'd notice that it simply looks to be around three thousand square feet and has six unusual window treatments. If you were looking at your body, what would you see?

By staying present to the simple fact of your Self in the mirror, neither liking nor disliking what you see, you'll begin to appreciate your body in a way you never did before. When I did this, I began by noting my brown skin, dark hair, full lips, and two brown eyes. I stayed present to what I was seeing and, eventually, I also started noting that I could see beauty with those eyes, feel gentle breezes on that skin and hair, taste delicious foods with that mouth. My body is a miracle in the world and the means to having a fulfilling life.

This was the beginning of ceasing to judge my Self for binging and purging, and of starting on the path to a healthier body. I'm not saying this was easy. When I tried looking in the mirror and telling my Self, *I am beautiful*, it was almost impossible. This statement felt extremely inauthentic and uncomfortable. Had I known what I learned in time, I would have changed the statement slightly, to say, *I really wish that I saw my Self as beautiful.* This would have allowed my intent to manifest a positive effect earlier. Yet, I got there just the same.

Just as I did, you may learn that by truly accepting the body you came in with, the only body you will ever have, your need to fix your Self with dieting, exercise, and even surgery, can fade away. Instead of fixing your body, you will nurture it, caring for it with kind thoughts, healthy food, and enjoyable, rather than driven, exercise.

Living happily with your body can be just this simple. The way you think about your body allows you to live with it harmoniously, in alignment with who you truly are. Once I was able to do this, I could finally feel that, like the women whose looks I once envied, I too was beautiful. And this did not lead to further comparisons. My outside now matched my inside, and I was able to simply enjoy feeling beautiful and being who I am. Accepting your body is an essential step in learning to love your Self and Be You.

Of course, the outside world doesn't help with this practice, for both males and females. Hollywood offers a very limiting view of beauty that is reflected in advertisements featuring skinny, big-boobed, highly sexualized women, and super-masculine, buffed-out guys, the goddesses and gods who exist to sell us products.

Gender roles are also still very much with us, in a society where boys are encouraged to be tough and hold back their feelings, and girls are expected to be beautiful no matter what they are feeling or doing. Girls must grow up to be successful and smart, hold down a full-time job, and be a full-time mother, who keeps a clean house. They must do this all at the same time, and now with the added obligation of always having to look hot.

It was a sad day for me when my then seven-year-old son, who would always point out beautiful flowers and trees on our walks, announced that boys aren't supposed to like flowers. He'd heard this from a classmate and, although I explained that no else could tell him what to like or feel, the damage was done. He'd been judged and felt the disconnection between the boy he really was and the boy he'd been told to be.

Then there's the matter of our values. We're taught that in order to be happy we need a good education, plenty of money, a successful marriage, and also, great clothes and cars. There is some truth in these messages, but they make too many of us lose our sense of Self-worth and look outward, rather than inward, for acknowledgement and acceptance. We are not the cars we drive or the shoes we wear, nor do our deepest feelings of Self-worth come from our social status or bank-account balances, who we've married, or our children and the success of our children. The greater truth is that, once we go beyond Self-limiting definitions of happiness and success, we can become who we intrinsically are. It is enough just to Be You, present to the fact of your potential.

When you think about your beliefs, ask yourself: are they truly my own, or did I absorb them from someone else, from the collective [un]consciousness or group mindedness? Were they imposed by the media, family, lovers, or friends? Am I putting aside my true desires and passions to please someone else? Am I playing it safe because I've been told that taking a chance on my dreams would be futile and distract me from practical matters like owning a car or a house? These are especially important questions to ask if you're a young woman or man growing up in our society.

Thinking Be You is a mindful daily practice that requires some discipline. Since everything begins as a thought, you need to stay aware of what you're thinking, both to combat negative judgments and manifest your intentions. It can help to remember that Thinking Be You begins with the intent to accept, honor, embrace, respect, and love your Self. That you are not your history or what anyone has labeled you; and that you want to be the best possible You and allow others to be their best, too. I ask you to be open to this belief: *You are worthy and deserving. You have limitless potential. And so does everyone else.*

How to Shut Down Limiting Thought-Forms and Replace Them with Authentic Affirmations

Here is a short list of Self-limiting thought forms and ways to transform them:

Self-limiting Thought-Forms:	New Thought-Forms
I am not enough.	My belief about my Self is limiting my experience in life. I am changing this belief and desire to see the truth about my Self as a capable human being.
I am not worthy.	This belief about my Self is not true and was taught to me by someone else's limited perspective about who they are and my potential. I am determined to know my Self worth.
I am not pretty enough, smart enough, old enough, young enough, etc.	I am tired of thinking this way about my Self. I want to shut off the voice inside of me that limits my perception of my Self. I am open to loving my Self.
It's not practical for me to chase after my dream.	I am no longer interested in living in fear and holding back my truest desires and passion. I am capable of pursuing and making my dreams come to fruition, and take care of my needs.

I'm not good at anything.	This belief about my Self is not true and was taught to me by someone else's limited perspective about who they are and my potential. I am excited to experience life and will no longer hold my Self back from doing what I desire.
I don't trust myself.	I am learning the truth about who I am as a human being. I have not trusted my Self in the past, and have just learned how amazing and perfect I actually am. I embrace my Self and will learn to listen to my inner voice and trust that no matter what the outcome, it was meant to give me an experience I can only grow and learn from.
I knew I wouldn't be good at this.	I will give everything I choose in life my best effort from a place of inner strength. As a human being I am capable of overcoming all hardship and my own self-doubt and fear. I am fearless.

No one would take me seriously. I have never been able to [fill in the blank]	I am willing to accept that my past actions may give a limited perception of who I really am. I will move forward with grace and strength to fulfill my own path. I only answer to my Self.
I'm always broke. I don't have enough money.	I am not a reflection of my bank account or material possessions. I am an abundant being, which allows me to access my creativity to manifest whatever I desire.
I don't have enough time.	I release all scarcity thinking and replace that with trust. My desires will manifest as I give them focused attention and intention. I am abundant.
My mother (father, sister, friend, teacher) was right; I'm not going to amount to anything.	I refuse to allow the limited perception that others have about me to influence the truth about who I really am. I offer them compassion for not knowing who we each are. I am forgiveness.

I am not creative.	As I am is all I need. Being free of self-judging thoughts allows my creative nature to flow through me. My creativity comes in all forms, I am open to my creative flow.

A Word About Writing

Thinking Be You takes place mostly in your head, but it can also take place in writing, with very good results. I'd like to recommend a powerful writing exercise that I found in The Artist's Way, by Julia Cameron. This well-known book on releasing creativity advocates starting with journaling, something I'd never felt like doing because I thought it was too cookie-cutter. After all, we each had our own ways of getting our thoughts out and so far, writing wasn't mine.

I later realized I was not a fan of journaling because I wasn't ready to confront what could be inside me. I was afraid to see what might come out and, more important, I thought it wouldn't matter even if I did. So what if I wrote about what I was thinking? How could that possibly help me feel better about a situation that wasn't going to change? As a very troubled teen, I'd resented my strict parents. What would writing about that have changed? What would it have changed about my fear, as a young adult, that my abusive boyfriend would carry out his threat to harm my family? Now, a little older, married with a kid, I was deeply in debt and had just lost a business. What good would it do to write about that?

It was at this point, as I was desperately trying to figure out what to do next, that I finally resorted to journaling. I'd try stream-of-consciousness writing; how could it hurt?

The technique is to commit to writing a single page and to just keep writing, no matter what, until you've done that. (Of course, if you'd like, you can always write more.) If you start feeling stuck part-way through the page, you just keep writing, whatever you are thinking, even if it's only, *This is stupid. I can't think of anything to write. What am I going to make for dinner? Why is my mind so empty? Why is the fridge empty? Why is my bank account empty? What is the point?*

The idea is to unload all your thoughts whether or not they make sense. The reason for this kind of writing is to free up your mind, declutter it so that your creativity can flow again. I was full of thoughts I wanted to get rid of, mostly having to do with doom, self-doubt, and destruction. And I wanted to shed them so I could come up with a game plan for getting out of debt and possibly starting another business. I was determined to help my small family out of the mess that I'd created. I wrote and wrote, wrote some more, and finally, I began to get ideas.

I still journal today. Whenever I need a good answer, I type out a question to my Self and wait for my Self to figure it out. First, all the garbage pours out. Then, inevitably, so do answers—wise answers that have always been inside me. So, if you dare, start putting your thoughts down on paper and expect to feel better. You may have to express a lot of grief, pain and hurt, but afterward comes calm, peace and relief. You've just released thoughts and beliefs that were hiding your inner light, and the more such thoughts you can get rid of, the closer you will come to the wonderful essence of your Self. Don't be shocked when new, fresh ideas, or maybe a poem or painting, appear. It's only natural for your creativity to flow out into the world, leaving you feeling what can only be described as Self-fulfillment.

Remember this once again: You are perfect and amazing as you are. Full of potential and possibility no matter what anyone else thinks or believes. If it's true that we are what we believe, why not choose to believe that you are nothing less than perfect?

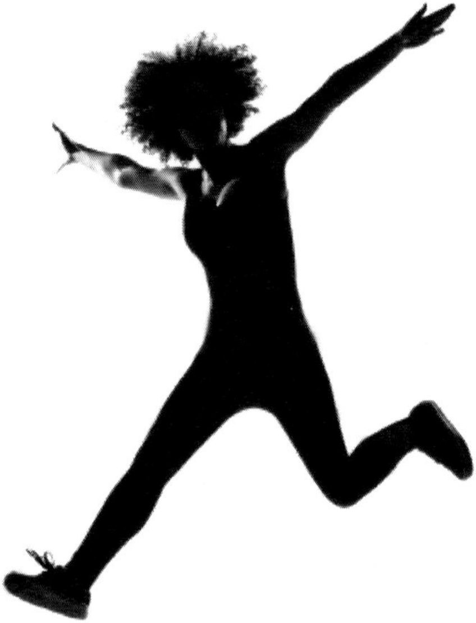

Speaking Be You

Thinking Be You leads directly to Speaking Be You. It's important to note that both of these practices ask you to believe in your Self as you are—when stripped of your story (the one you tell about yourself, and what you suspect others are telling about you), your past experiences, and all the things you think are wrong with you. Be You is a lifestyle, and the practices in this book are aimed at helping you unlearn all your past negative programming.

Beneath all your issues, you truly are an astounding human being with the potential to have all you desire. You've probably never had anyone tell you that on a consistent basis or speak to you very often as the wonderful being you really are. That's what Speaking Be You is all about.

Speaking Be You is using the language of love and total acceptance, the spoken language of the heart. It's the way we all desire to be spoken to and communicated with. Can you imagine feeling validated, heard, and able to express how you truly feel without the fear of being judged or shamed? I never thought it was possible until I learned how it actually can be done. Like Thinking Be You, Speaking Be You requires you to accept who you are, and put who you are into action. The more you do this, the easier it becomes to accept others and to be okay when they are not accepting of who you are.

Learning to speak Be You requires you to think before you speak, to take more time to say what you really want to express, and to speak with clarity. Most importantly, you learn how to be completely present to the person who is speaking to you. This allows you to hold that person in a safe emotional space if there is conflict.

The practices I am sharing with you are based on teachings that I have learned from many others and integrated into an ongoing lifestyle. Let's start with how to speak from what I've called your natural state of being, the powerful, abundant, creative, and loving state that is everyone's inner power source. As I learned through Howard Falco's inspiring book, *I Am: The Power of Discovering Who You Really Are*, it's enough simply to say those two words:

I am.

Saying *I am* asserts your being and makes you present in the world. You can say, *I am a student, I am happy, I am sad.* Saying *I am* states your truth and creates a direct connection between your Self and others. It also leads to knowing Who I am and Who I can be.

This sounds simple, I know. But think how often we counter our truth with limiting words, like the three-letter word, not. Imagine saying: *I'm not … I can't … I haven't … I don't …*

What just happened? You cut your Self off at the knees is what happened. You defined your Self as lacking instead of as a powerful, abundant, creative, and loving human being with a full set of feelings and capabilities.

So, here's the practice: Speak from your power source I am and, when you do, try using the tool of removing words of scarcity from your vocabulary. It doesn't always make grammatical sense to do so, but bearing this in mind, do it as often as you can. These words include not and all its variations, especially don't, haven't, won't and can't.

When I first decided to remove these words from my vocabulary, I was determined to live a powerful life filled with positivity and wanted other people to experience such a life too. Why? I was pregnant and wanted to speak to my future child as if he had the potential to be anything—without limits. I didn't want to simply hand him whatever I could; I knew from my own experience that the best gift I could provide was that of knowing him—as whatever he was born to be. I adopted this practice from a desire to speak in ways that would empower him, even when I needed him not to do something, for the sake of his safety or well-being.

For example, I wanted to avoid saying: *Don't touch that. Don't do that. You can't have that. You can't watch that. You can't eat that.*

Doing this might sound impractical, even impossible, but if you take it as a challenge, your creative and compassionate Self will come up with more empowering ways to communicate. *Don't touch that* becomes, *Be careful, that's sharp, and you might hurt your self.* And *Don't do that* becomes, *Baby, please step down from the coffee table. I'm concerned you might fall.* The second example is an illustration of a two-for-one statement, in which you first give a clear, direct request and then an authentic expression of your feeling in that moment. When you make statements like this, you communicate with clarity and keep your Self present with the other person in that moment.

Now let's switch back to your Self. You may often start sentences with: *I don't ... I can't ... I won't ... I haven't ...*

Doing this creates statements of lack. How can you replace them with powerful *I am* statements? When I first committed to this practice, I was frustrated because I noticed I spoke from lack most of the time. So, first, be patient with your Self. And if possible, write down lack-statements whenever you catch your Self saying them, to help you figure out more empowering ways of making the same points later. Here are some common statements of lack and suggestions for replacing them:

Self-limiting statements ...	I am empowered ...
I can't think of how to do it.	I'm having a hard time coming up with how to do it.
I can't believe how [fill in the blank]	I'm shocked ... I'm surprised ... I'm baffled ...
I dunno.	I have no idea and could care less. I have no idea and now I'm curious. Let me Google that. I wish I could answer that.

I can't meet you later.	I already made plans.
I don't remember.	I forgot.
I can't say.	I promised to keep it a secret.
I wouldn't dare.	I have no desire to do that. I prefer to be safe.

Note that often when we start sentences with Self-limiting words, we can simply turn them into statements that express our feelings, as with the example, *I can't believe*, which becomes more powerful when stated as *I'm shocked/surprised/baffled...*

What to Do About Woulda, Coulda, Shoulda

Remember these? We often speak away our true power by using these expressions, which convey regrets, Self-judgment or judgment toward another.

Say the following sentences out loud to your Self:

I should have taken the other way. I should've told him I how really felt. I could've done a better job. I would've been on time, but I slept in.

Notice how these statements make you feel smaller and less powerful. They can hurt, and if you're sensitive enough, can even feel like a form of violence against your Self. They sound even worse when you imagine someone saying them to you:

You should've taken the other way!
You should've told him how you really felt.
You could've done a better job.
You would've been on time, but you slept in.

So, how can you express your Self without using should've, could've, and would've? The best way is to express your regrets and disappointment directly, with positive *I Am* statements that keep your Self front and center. It's definitely okay to feel regrets and disappointment, and, in fact, you need to know what you're feeling if want to move ahead. Once you do, you need to get these feelings outside you, cleanly and clearly, so you no longer feel their impact. Releasing them allows you to get to your inner truth. You can think of the process as one of clearing clutter from your house or weeding a beautiful garden. Your garden's lovely flowers and trees are always there; it's just a lot easier to enjoy them when you remove the weeds and trim the lawn.

Here is a list of commonly used Self-limiting statements that use woulda, coulda, and shoulda and ways to change them:

Self-limiting statements	I feel …
I should've taken the other way.	I'm so mad at myself for not taking the other way!
I should've told him how I really feel.	I'm disappointed with my Self for holding back my feelings.
I could've done a better job.	I'm disappointed with the work that I produced.
I would've been on time, if I hadn't slept in.	I'm tired of being late.

Be Aware of Negative, Limiting, Absolute Statements

Speaking Be you is about always accessing our power and limitless potential—or, whenever we can. One way we often limit ourselves is by using negative absolutes to describe a situation. It's one thing to affirm your Self by saying, *I am always accessing my inner power*, which is really a statement of intent, and another thing to limit your Self by saying, *I'm always late*, which is supposedly a statement of fact. A negative absolute statement may feel like an accurate expression of Self in the moment; however, upon further thought, usually turns out to be inaccurate.

When we live Be You, we intend to honor the power source of ourselves and others—insofar as we can. Negative absolute statements have the effect of limiting that source and thus our potential. When spoken to us, such statements often trigger our anger and we tend to react defensively. Do any of these sound familiar?

You're always late.

You never leave me messages.

Everyone thinks you're lazy.

Nobody cares what you think.

You have to do that before you go.

You must get good grades to go to a good college.

You always forget your lunch.

The absolute truth about negative absolute statements is that they just might be preventing someone from realizing her true potential. Even if she has arrived five minutes late for a meeting, for the last ten meetings, does this really mean she will always be late? And does saying she is always late help her to believe she can be on time? What motivation does she have to be on time if you—or you and everyone else in the meeting—believes she will always be late? She doesn't. And the same applies to you, if you're the person who is habitually late.

Instead, tell the person how you feel about them being late. An example would be:

I notice that lately when you meet me for lunch or dinner, that you have been running late. The first few times, I understood why and I know that things happen, yet I feel frustrated because I take time out of my day to meet with you, or I had things that I could have completed if I had known you were going to be late. And then you can make a request: In the future, if you know you're going to be late, please let me know and if you think you're going to be more than twenty minutes late, it's probably best for us to reschedule.

Therefore, be mindful of using limiting, negative absolutes when speaking about your Self and others. Elevate the tone of your language and sprinkle your communications with authentic compassionate communication where you can express your needs rather than shame and judgment.

When Speaking Be You to Others

You empower your Self when you say, *I am*...

And when speaking to and about other people, you empower them when you say, *You are*...

If you notice that you are not speaking in a positive fashion, are putting other people down and pointing out flaws about them, this is usually a very strong indicator that you are not feeling love and compassion toward your Self. It's time to go inward and see how you are feeling about your Self when you notice that behavior.

Remember that Speaking Be You is about using language that comes from our inner power source of possibility. If you are seeing flaws and feeling discomfort with others, it's also time to look inward at your needs, and then do your best to see what the other person's needs are, too.

Practice speaking from your inner power source first, and you will naturally shift your language when speaking to others, to hold them within their own inner power source.

Practice makes perfect, and over time, you will replace more and more habits of limited speaking with habits that empower your Self and others.

Replace Trying with Doing Your Best

You're an amazing and fully capable human being. So, as you undertake this practice, I ask you to stop trying to do things, and instead do your best. If you want to get better at something, just keep practicing, doing your best, and giving it your all. Let's give this a test run, as you read the following: *Just give it a try.* Now read this: *Do your best!* A good expectation to hold for your Self is that whatever you do will be your best. And don't be attached to the outcome of your best. Just give what you're doing your best. Tell your Self and others that's what you're doing, then do it and feel good about it.

The Practice of Nonviolent, Compassionate Communication

I've given a lot of examples for elevating limiting language, and now wish to talk about the practice of nonviolent, compassionate communication as set forth by Marshall Rosenberg. After I explain the basics, I'll provide more examples of Speaking Be You, based on his model. For more information on this practice, which is all about speaking with compassion toward your Self and others, I highly recommend that you read Marshall's book, *Nonviolent Communication: A Language of Life*, and that you visit his website, www.cnvc.org, to order books and audio tapes and even locate a practice group or coach to help you with your practices. You can also create a user login at the site to access training material and educational content.

How to Speak from Your Heart

The model for nonviolent communication, communicating in a way that is conscious and compassionate, is very simple and straightforward. Yet, like the rest of the ideas in this book, practicing it can be challenging, especially if you are in conflict with someone. When you're in conflict, even if some of your exchanges have been verbally violent, it's extra-important to remember to be gentle to your Self and give your Self compassion, too.

When I began practicing the model, one of my greatest revelations was that I was able to remain calm, even when other people were expressing anger, disappointment, and judgment—toward me. This was a very big deal. The more I practiced, the more I was able to free myself from taking their negative remarks personally. I realized that when people communicate with each other, and even more when they're afraid to, they usually believe they will be judged, wronged, misunderstood, blamed, aroused to anger, or be the cause of anger.

And here's the *aha!*, I understood that we all feel uncomfortable when others are expressing their negative feelings because we can barely deal with our own, let alone someone else's. I then realized it was through the practice of self-acceptance and authentic expression, which opens up our natural state of being, that I was able to withstand other people's negative feelings even when I was the target.

It just happens when my heart is open and I am in a place of acceptance and compassion. Does this mean I am calm and feel only compassion? Not at all. I still get angry and frustrated, yet by keeping my heart open and discerning the needs of both parties, the communication remains authentic. Staying authentic might mean that both parties have uncomfortable feelings, yet at least are able to express themselves and be part of a compassionate communication process that includes honesty and empathy.

Using nonviolent communication does not require that the other party know what you are doing, or even wish to speak to you compassionately. If your sole intent is to give and receive compassionately, and you do all you can to communicate your motive, the process has a way of becoming mutual.

I have a lot more to learn about nonviolent communication, yet what I have learned to date has had a profound impact on my life. Nonviolent communication is a lifelong practice. There are many aspects that Marshall shares, and a few that really stand out for me include:

- The model for nonviolent communication—a process with four components and two parts
- No compromising – if both parties compromise, no one's needs are met
- Using language authentically
- Learning the difference between feelings and thoughts/beliefs/judgments
- Having compassion for your Self

The Essentials for Authentic and Compassionate Be You Speak

Here are the basics of Marshall's model for compassionate communication. The four components include:

1. Observing: Observation without evaluation consists of noticing concrete things and actions around us, such as facts about the situation we are observing. This practice helps us identify concrete things and what feelings we have about those concrete things, and to be in the present moment, without blaming or judging.

2. Understanding and Expressing Feelings: When we notice things around us, we inevitably experience different emotions and physical sensations in each particular moment. Distinguishing feelings from judging thoughts and beliefs is an essential step in the compassionate communication process.

3. Identifying and Expressing Needs: All individuals have needs and values that sustain and enrich their lives. When those needs are met, we experience comfortable feelings, like happiness or peacefulness, and when they are not, we experience uncomfortable ones, like frustration, fear, and anger. Understanding that we, as well as those around us, have many needs is the most important step in learning to practice compassion and empathy.

4. Requesting: To make clear requests, rather than demands, is crucial and comes from understanding our own needs and the needs of others. When we learn to request concrete actions that can be carried

out in the present moment, we begin to find ways to cooperatively and creatively ensure that everyone's needs are met.

The two parts of nonviolent communication are:

1. Empathy: Receiving communication empathically, with the heart, creates a means to connect with others and share experiences in a truly life-enriching way. Empathy allows us to put ourselves into another's shoes to sense their feelings and needs; in essence, it is being open and available to what is alive in others. It also gives us the means to remain present to and aware of our own needs along with the needs of others, even in extreme situations that are often difficult to handle.

2. Self-Honesty to Bring About Compassion: Giving compassionately, from the heart, has its root in honesty with ourselves. Such honesty begins with truly understanding our feelings and needs, and being in tune with what is alive in ourselves in the present moment. When we learn to give ourselves empathy, we can start to break down the barriers to communication that keep us from connecting with others.

From these four components and two parts, Marshall has created a model for life-enhancing communication that can be highly effective in solving conflict with our family members, with our friends, with our coworkers, and with ourselves. The basic outline of the model is the following:

When I see _____
I feel _____
Because my need for _____ is not met.
Would you be willing to _____?

Keep in mind that this is just a model, designed to allow for flexibility of expression in the moment. When I first tried using it, I sounded phony to myself because I was not used to following its form and suggestions for using language. The examples that follow are meant to show you how the model can work in action. With practice, you'll be able to integrate all four of the components with empathy and self-honesty without having to think about following the form. I still refer to the form, however, when I need to work through something really important that's happening in my life.

Here's the first example: When I was younger and had to do homework, I preferred to do it as soon as possible after school, and my mother made a point of telling me that if I did, I could then do whatever I wanted. If you are still a student, let's imagine that like mine, your mother prefers that you do your homework right away, and unlike me, you would rather not. A compassionate communication between the two of you might go something like this:

Mom: How about getting your homework out of the way, right after you have a snack?

You: I don't want to do my homework now. I don't have that much, and I'd rather do it later.

Mom: Well, if you don't have that much homework, why not do it now?

You: I just told you, I don't want to, why do I have to? Isn't what matters is that I have it done by tomorrow?

So, what's going on here? Some might think your mom is being too lenient and that you're talking back and should just do what she says. But she might be parenting in a different way, trying to give you respect for knowing your own needs even though she'd rather you did it her way. Right now she is cutting you some slack, as she chooses to step back and consider both your needs. As she tries to figure out your needs, this might allow you to say:

You: Mom, I'm at school all day, I just want to come home, have a snack, and take a break from school stuff. I promise I'll do my homework later.

Mom might then give you empathy and validation:

Mom: Okay, I'm sorry. I was thinking that you might want to get it out of the way. Of course you deserve to take a break from school stuff. (She then expresses her own need.) I guess I need to make sure you give yourself enough time to finish it. Okay, I'm fine with this. I know you know what you need to do. (Then she makes her request.) Would you be willing to give me a heads up when you're either starting it or finishing it?

And you might then say:

You: I guess.

Thinking, *hey, good enough for me*, Mom might then add to her request:

Mom: May I suggest you get it completed no later than 8:00 p.m. and, on days when you have swim class, before you leave for class, say start at 5:00 p.m.?

This sounds reasonable, so you say:

You: Yes.

Mom: Great. Thank you. I'm proud that that you're being responsible enough to complete your homework and take care of yourself, too.

In this conversation, both of your needs have been met. Mom has empowered you by trusting that you know your own requirements and has realized she no longer needs you to do your homework immediately to allay her fear that you won't finish it. The outcome is happy for both parties. There is a lot going on in this discussion, primarily the enacting of:

- Speaking from a source of power to another person's source of power
- Accepting and respecting another person's needs and desires
- Compassion, empathy and honesty

The How to Be You Handbook

- Trust

Imagine the shoe is on the other foot. You're babysitting your little brother and are responsible for getting him to complete his homework. But he doesn't realize how long it's going to take him, gets frustrated, and ends up crying. Here's how you might deal with him compassionately.

You: Hey, what's going on?

Notice that you have refrained from asking, what's wrong? Our society is not comfortable with having uncomfortable feelings and often labels those who have them wrong. With compassionate and authentic expression, there is nothing wrong with expressing feelings, even if you're a boy.

Little bro: (still crying) Nothing!

You: Nothing? Really? It's obvious to me that you're upset. What's going on, honey?

Little bro: Nothing!!

You: (Now, you choose to open your heart, use some intuition, and give empathy and compassion to your crying brother.) Okay. I'm concerned because I see you crying. I see that you've got your school work out, and I also see that it's way past 8:00 p.m. I think you might be worried I'm going to get mad and, at the same time, you have a lot more work to do and you're feeling overwhelmed. If that's how you're feeling, I want to help you, okay?

Little bro: (looking relieved, putting his guard down) Okay.

You: You can take all the time you need.

Then when he finishes his homework, you might say:

You: I see you're finished. Do you feel relieved now that it's done?

Little bro: Yeah.

You: Is there something you can do next time, to make sure you have enough time?

Little bro: Look over my homework earlier to see if there might be a lot to do.

After a conversation like this, you may notice that your little brother starts on his homework a bit earlier than usual. He is happy that you have not chosen to tell him he made what others might call a mistake. Nor did you use this situation as an opportunity to force your will on him in the future. The best thing you can do as an older sister or parent is to keep seeing a child as a wise individual who knows how to work through anything that comes up in life.

Now it's time for a disclaimer. When I started this practice, I unconsciously hoped that it would prove a new means of letting me get my way. I soon came to understand, however, that compassionate communication is all about equality, as two people express and attempt to get their needs met. I appreciate Marshall's wisdom in saying that emotional pain is a signal of unmet needs. It takes a lot of courage to face the pain that points to your own needs, and patience to accept that even if you can express them, they may not be met. In fact, getting them met sometimes requires "giving in." And this brings up the topic of:

No compromises

It seems counter-intuitive to say, as a friend once did, that in nonviolent communication, there can be no compromise. This was just her way of observing that in a practice based on everyone's needs being met, compromise results in both parties' needs being only partially met. Compromise is in fact often possible in compassionate communication, yet sometimes one person's needs can only be met at the other person's expense. In this case, one party may end the stand-off by compassionately giving the other person what he/she needs. The party who gives appears to be giving up her/his needs, when actually he or she is replacing them with a need to give. With practice, you may find that you can become the giver on occasion.

As an example, here's what could happen between a wife and husband, or roommates. Imagine you're the woman. You've lived on your own and have always enjoyed having a clean kitchen, especially right after dinner. You hate waking up to dirty dishes in the sink. Now you live with your fiancé. He works from home and has an extremely heavy workload.

You: You know, I'd really appreciate it if we could wash the dishes after dinner. In fact, after every meal.

Him: Sorry, you know how busy I am. I barely have time to go to the bathroom, I'm on so many calls. It's hard to find time to even rinse a dish.

You: Fine, but what about me? I really appreciate a clean kitchen, and I need you to help me out with this.

Him: I would love to help you out—because that would mean I don't have a crazy workload. But all that would do is cause me more stress. I'm sorry, I don't want to tell you that I'll even try because I know that all that matters to me during the day is that I need to get work done.

You: Okay, but what about after dinner? We eat late, and you're usually not working by then any more.

Him: Are you kidding? By then I don't want to do anything. After dinner I just want to chill and watch my shows.

You: Every time I see an unrinsed dish in the sink, I feel resentful and like you don't appreciate what I do.

Him: I'm sorry you feel that way. I know you work hard too. My choosing not to do the dishes doesn't mean I don't appreciate you, but I'm not the one who cares about dishes in the sink. So even if I rinse them and put them in the dishwasher, I'll probably start feeling resentful too because I'm not relaxing. How about I do them before going to bed?

You: I don't like waiting that long because then I don't get to relax for the rest of the night. I can't relax knowing the dishes aren't washed.

In this conversation, both people are expressing their needs, but neither one is going to get them met. Now imagine that you, as this woman, step back to think more about the situation. You realize that you know your fiancé loves you, that his job is just as stressful as he says, and that the last thing you want to do is cause him more stress, or to feel resentful. You decide you will no longer ask him to do the dishes, but do request that he at least try to rinse them. You also decide that when you see unwashed dishes you will no longer feel resentful but will instead think, *Yes, he's super-busy and stressed. Since I need to have a clean kitchen, I'm willing to take care of it for both of us, just like he's willing to work hard to take care of both of us.*

The outcome might be less tension, due to a clean kitchen and occasional effort on the part of your fiancé to rinse a dish. When he does make the effort, you can say thank you, and mean it. You also realize that some day, the situation may be reversed. You may be the one working nonstop, and he just might clean the kitchen for both of you, even though he doesn't care about seeing dishes in the sink.

Here's an example of a boyfriend situation in which it can feel dangerous to express how you feel.

You: I have something I want to talk to you about, only I'm afraid that you'll think I'm being silly or paranoid or jealous. I'm not; it just bothers me.

Boyfriend: Okay, what is it? Please tell me.

You: I've noticed that my friend likes to be all over you. She gets really touchy-feely, and I don't like it. It seems to make you uncomfortable, too.

Boyfriend: I know, I do feel uncomfortable when she does it, and I'm sorta shocked that she does it in front of you, which makes me wonder if she doesn't mean it in that way.

You: I know, I thought the same thing. I wonder if she knew that it bothered me, if she'd keep doing it?

Boyfriend: If it bothers you that much, I will ask her to stop. The reason I haven't is because she's your friend, and I didn't want to make things weird between you.

You: Well, before you do that, let me talk to her. I think I just really wanted to know how you felt, first.

Now you need the courage to speak to your girlfriend:

You: Hey, I really want to talk to you about something that's bothering me and, at the same time, I don't want you to feel bad. I just want to be able to talk to you about it.

Girlfriend: Okay, what's going on?

You: I feel really silly because you and I are good friends, and I don't want to assume anything if you don't mean anything by it.

Girlfriend: I'm already feeling funny about this. Tell me quick.

You: All right, I'll just say it. I feel uncomfortable when you hug my boyfriend so much and rub his back. Do I need to be concerned that you're coming on to him?

Girlfriend: OMG! I'm so sorry, I don't mean that at all. I guess I just want him to like me because you do, but not like that. I'm really sorry.

You: No, it's fine. I just wanted to make sure that I told you because I didn't want to assume, and my boyfriend wasn't sure what to make of your actions either.

Girlfriend: I'll be sure to apologize to him. And I'll respect the boundary.

And here's one more example of a compassionate communication you might have with your daughter, with whom you have a good relationship.

Mom: I friended you on Facebook, why won't you friend me back?

You: Debbie's mom writes embarrassing stuff on her wall all the time and uses it to check up on her. I don't want you to be on my Facebook.

Mom: It sounds like you need reassurance that I won't write embarrassing stuff on your wall, is that true?

You: Yeah, I guess.

Mom: If I promised not to do that, would you friend me back?

You: Yes, but the minute you do anything sneaky or embarrassing, I'm unfriending you, even though you're my mother.

Now that you've read the examples, let's revisit the model for compassionate communication:

Observing, Understanding Feelings, Identifying and Expressing Needs, and Requesting. As you've seen, the steps don't always have to be done in order. Sometimes you might express a feeling about an observation and go straight to the request. For example, you might say, I'm frustrated because the dishes are left in the sink when you agreed to do them. Will you please clean them before you go out with your friends?

Here's a little more about the model:

Observing

We have feelings about everything we experience. I like to refer to observations as the part of the experience that cannot be disputed, like unwashed dishes left in the sink. Both parties agree that there are unwashed dishes in the sink, but feel differently about them being unwashed. They also have different needs that might have nothing to do with the dishes.

Understanding and Expressing Feelings

When they first practice compassionate communication, many people have no idea how to express their feelings, because they don't know what a feeling actually is. For example, you might tell someone, *I feel like you're ignoring me*. This is an interpretation of the other person's action rather than a clear statement of your feeling. You might feel hurt, because you wanted the other person's attention. A clearer statement of your feeling might be, *I felt hurt the other day; I thought you might have been ignoring me.*

To reverse the situation, when practicing compassionate communication with someone who's not familiar with it, you can help that person express feelings by offering cues. If a person says, *I felt like you were ignoring me the other day*, you might reply, *Oh, you must have felt hurt and shocked if that's what you thought. I'm sorry, I'm certain I didn't see you.*

Identifying and Expressing Needs

Understanding your needs and those of others immediately puts you in compassion mode, helping you to disarm any conflict that may be occurring. Your heart opens up, and now you're playing detective with the desire to resolve the conflict. When you open your heart to solve a problem, following this model, the outcome will pleasantly surprise you.

Requesting

As I've mentioned before, as natural powerful beings, it is our nature to be loving and compassionate. When we can identify our own needs and the needs of others, it's easier to formulate a request and ask others if they are willing to fulfill it. Most of the time, you'll find that you can come to a resolution, even if it only means agreeing to disagree.

To sum up, here is the recommended list of practices for Speaking Be You, to keep you speaking at your highest level:

- Speak from your inner power source and always access your highest level by keeping your I Am statements pure. This includes removing, where possible, the word not and all forms of it, including can't, don't, won't, couldn't, shouldn't and wouldn't.

- Be mindful of limiting statements and replace them with empowering ones. (Look back to the chart on p. 64.)
- And be mindful of how you are expressing your feelings. (See the chart on p. 67.)
- Replace *try* with *will do my best*.
- Speak from the heart, using the model for compassionate communication as a tool for conflict resolution and for connecting more deeply with your peers, family, colleagues and community.

Living Be You

Living Be You is a constant mindful practice of keeping everything in your life in alignment with the truth about who you are. When you are Thinking and Speaking Be You, you are Living Be You. It becomes a lifestyle.

Just as you can change your diet to feed your body with nutritious foods, you will become conscious of filling your thoughts about your Self and others with love, compassion, and feelings of worthiness. The more that you do, the more you will find that you are patient, free of judgment, and able to have compassion for others as they express themselves, whether or not they are trying to live according to the principles of Be You. You will become able to see other people's pure potential, even if they do not, and will be able to hold a safe place for them in which to express themselves.

You'll notice that when you watch television or films, read the news, or talk with others, that you'll be able to see the limiting thought-forms that are present. This awareness might bring up feelings of loneliness and even sadness, as you notice how many there are who limit their potential and that of others. The best solution is simply to model what Living Be You speaks and acts like, and share your feelings and insights when an opportunity arises. A perfect example of this is watching television commercials or seeing any ads that depict very specific gender roles that perpetuate the limiting beliefs and roles of females and males. Often we will see a certain kind of beauty–women who are skinny and who are dressed in revealing clothes to sell products. And men are portrayed as muscular and competitive. You even notice it in toy commercials. Girls are programmed early on to look and behave a certain way to get attention. And boys are taught to hold their feelings in, be strong and like fast cars. How can these messages and images continue in a world so advanced in technology? Our youth, more than ever, are being bullied in cruel ways including cyber bullying. I feel sad when I see how slow the progress is toward acceptance of self and others. Now with this knowledge and awareness, you will be able to point out the limiting messages. It will astound you how often and prevalent it is in our society. It's time to live Be You and reverse and deprogram from untruths about who we each are.

Living Be You in your physical body will allow you to stop desperately trying to fix your Self through diets and exercise. Now you will eat and work out because you want to take care of your Self. You'll exercise for the joy of being active and will enjoy what you eat, guilt-free. You'll indulge in decadence and feel good, in control of what you consume while making overall healthy choices for your body.

You will notice greater inner peace as you live Be You. By eliminating negative, self-limiting thought-forms, all that will be left is to create and manifest the life you desire, while making deeper connections in your relationships. You will no longer have the need to fix other people because the need to fix your Self will dissipate. If you were a people pleaser, this too will pass. Your search for approval will be replaced with first giving love and compassion to your Self, so that you can provide a space for others to live the life that they choose.

When you live Be You, you will transcend feelings of self-righteousness, as you connect to your entire life experience. You might laugh as you find your Self noticing and appreciating sights you've walked or driven by for years without really seeing them.

You will experience a sense of freedom that you'll cherish and strive to keep. Becoming free of judging my Self and others felt like losing a huge burden. When it was gone, I felt lighter in every cell of my body.

As you begin Living Be You, enjoy the presence of who you are in every moment. Nothing else matters except realizing this truth, which is your birthright.

I am excited for you, as you prepare to meet and love one of the most amazing people you will ever know.

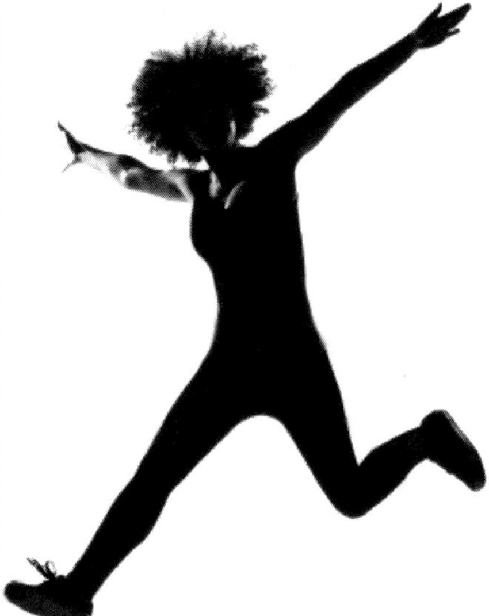

The Forty-Day Be You Program

Congratulations on embarking on an inward journey to find true love and happiness! It might sound idealistic and corny, but from my perspective, it's pretty much what happens when you take the time to treat your Self with love, respect, and compassion. This is what it mostly looks like when you accept, love, and trust your Self. There really is no other way for it to look or be!

Yes, we each have our own story and our own experiences, yet what it all boils down to is that we are each magnificent, and it is indeed our birthright to be happy. If you are willing to take a few moments to turn your old negative habits into new, positive practices, I promise that you'll get so hooked on the change you'll do everything possible to stay with it. Your happiness exists now, if you can trust that you are worthy and deserving of it and are open to experiencing it in this moment.

Performing the practices consistently, can transform you. Small, daily steps, taken mindfully, are what count.

This book ends with a forty-day Be You program designed to help you realize who you truly are and create a life that you deserve. It's based on the Ten Principles of Be You that you found on pgs. 21 - 24, in the section called How To Use This

Book, and it takes forty days because tradition has shown this is the length of time required to bring about a real change of consciousness.

Here's how it works: If you have not already taken the Be You Pledge on p. 20, you can do so now. It's then a good idea to commit to faithfully follow the forty-day Be You program each and every day—and if you miss even one, to start over and continue until you can complete the entire period. You are building up new energy as you complete the program, but it will dissipate if you take a break, so it's important to remain consistent.

During the program, you will read one Be You principle each day until you've read all ten, and then start over. This means you will go through the entire list four times during the forty-day period. When you complete the program, staying mindful of Thinking and Speaking Be You will keep the principles alive as you begin Living Be You.

As you begin the forty-day Be You program, here are a few reminders to guide you:

- Remember to keep an open mind.
- Be generous about opening up your heart to your Self.
- Remember to stay gentle with your Self. Expect to go back to old habits now and then, and when this

happens, or you miss a day of the program, give your Self renewed compassion and empathy.

To begin:

1. Establish a specific date to start your program, such as the beginning of a particular week. You can start on any day of the week, including today, if you're motivated to start immediately. Then simply count out forty days on your calendar from your start date and mark the completion date.

2. On the first day of the program, write the statement below in a journal specially dedicated to the program:

On this day, (date) I, (insert your name), cease believing that I am anything less than perfectly capable, worthy, and deserving of all that I desire. I cease believing that my body is ugly or unhealthy, that my life is going nowhere, that nothing good happens to me. I know that my experience in life has been a manifestation of my limiting beliefs. I surrender to my Self and embrace my entire body and the body of the universe of which I am a part. I accept that I am an abundant being that is creative and fully capable to produce and manifest that which I desire. I let go of the illusion of who I am that comes from others not knowing who they are and who I truly am. On this day, I renounce and release all limiting beliefs I hold unconsciously, including those that were created through collective unconsciousness. I am no longer limiting my Self. I acknowledge the inner power source inside of me that has longed to be set free from my limiting beliefs.

Choose to follow the program before going to bed or upon rising. After reading each daily principle, reread it as many times as you wish to fully understand and take on its meaning. Meditate on it, focusing with thoughtfulness and feeling on each of its ideas, and allow it to fill your consciousness. Following your meditation, use your journal to record whatever thoughts come to you. Please allow the entire process a minimum of fifteen minutes.

Here, again, are:

The Ten Principles of Be You

1. I am born with everything needed to fulfill my desires. The only things preventing me from fulfilling my desires are the subconscious thoughts and beliefs that counter this truth. I release all subconscious and conscious thoughts that prevent me from believing that I am less than perfect as I am in this moment.

2. I accept everything about myself, including my physical body, to the choices I have made in my

past experiences and any hurt and pain I may have caused others. I choose to speak gently about my Self and others.

3. I am grateful for my wonderful senses that allow me to see, hear, smell, taste, touch, and feel. I will notice my sensory experiences throughout this day and give thanks for each sense.

4. I allow my Self to Be and I allow others to Be. I only have to be responsible for my self and present to the existence of others. I have no need to be responsible for how others feel. I allow them to feel what they feel and I will authentically express my feelings and needs with them as we experience life with each other.

5. I am a human being capable of giving and receiving love. I do not label myself as good or bad; I am simply the essence of where possibility begins. This is true for my Self and for my fellow human beings. I choose to see my Self and others as worthy and deserving.

6. I am authentic. It is in my nature to have feelings and desires. I am capable of expressing my feelings and needs. I am capable of being present to the feelings and needs of others, and am able to look beyond any

limiting belief or illusion that someone may have about who I am or who they think they are.

7. I am compassionate. I am able to give compassion to my Self and others. I will listen with an open heart and be completely present to others. I will not be offended or take negative comments personally; this is an old practice that I am releasing and replacing with compassion.

8. I have the ability to overcome negative feelings including anger, resentment, despair, hate, loneliness and all forms of fear. When these feelings come up, I know they are there for me to resolve and heal, so that I can experience higher, positive feelings that expand my experience. I am capable of overcoming anything I put my attention to. I am fully capable, wise and strong.

9. I am here to experience loving relationships with others and know that I must have, or desire to have, a healthy and loving relationship with my Self. My relationships with others create opportunities to see my Self and to love my Self and others more deeply.

10. I surrender to the flow of love that resides within me. Love has always been with me. It has never been necessary for someone to give it to me, and I have not needed to receive love from someone else

in order to give it. I now open my heart and allow love to flow through me.

As mentioned, if you wish, you can accompany the forty-day program with the mindful practices of Thinking Be You and Speaking Be You. And when you complete the program, staying mindful of these practices will keep the Ten Principles of Be You shining like guiding lights, as you begin Living Be You.

May you enjoy every fruit of your being, as you join me in the practice of Be You!